BENNETT, Leonie

The life of George Cadbury

The Life of

George Cadbury

The famous chocolate maker

Leonie Bennett

Heinemann LIBRARY

www.heinemann.co.uk/library

Visit our website to find out more information about **Heinemann Library** books.

To order:

 Phone 44 (0) 1865 888066

 Send a fax to 44 (0) 1865 314091

Visit the Heinemann Bookshop at www.heinemann.co.uk/library to browse our catalogue and order online.

First published in Great Britain by Heinemann Library, Halley Court, Jordan Hill, Oxford OX2 8EJ, part of Harcourt Education.
Heinemann is a registered trademark of Harcourt Education Ltd.

Editorial: Lucy Thunder and Harriet Milles
Design: Richard Parker and
    Tinstar Design Ltd (www.tinstar.co.uk)
Picture Research: Melissa Allison and
Virginia Stroud-Lewis
Production: Camilla Smith

Originated by Repro Multi-Warna
Printed and bound in China by
    South China Printing Company

The paper used to print this book comes from sustainable resources.

ISBN 0 431 18105 5
09 08 07 06 05
10 9 8 7 6 5 4 3 2 1

British Library Cataloguing in Publication Data
Leonie Bennett
George Cadbury. – (The Life of)
338.7'6413374'092
A full catalogue record for this book is available from the British Library.

Acknowledgements
The Publishers would like to thank the following for permission to reproduce photographs:
pp. 4, 25a Harcourt Education Ltd./Tudor Photography and reproduced with the consent of Cadbury Ltd.; p. 5 Mary Evans Picture Library/Town & Country Planning; pp. 6, 7, 8, 14, 15, 18, 19, 24 Copyright Cadbury Trebor Bassett, reproduced courtesy of Birmingham City Archives; pp. 9, 11, 21 reproduced with the consent of Cadbury Ltd.; p. 10 K. Hackenberg/Zefa; pp. 12, 13 Getty Images/Hulton Archive; p. 16 Getty Images/Hulton Archive/Fox; pp. 17, 20, 25b The Advertising Archive Ltd.; pp. 22, 23 Getty Images/Hulton Archive/Topical; p. 26 Jonathan Berg/www.bplphoto.co.uk; p. 27 Philippa Lewis/Edifice

Cover photograph of George Cadbury, reproduced with permission of Birmingham Library Services.
Page icons: Harcourt Education/Tudor Photography.

Every effort has been made to contact copyright holders of any material reproduced in this book. Any omissions will be rectified in subsequent printings if notice is given to the Publishers.

Disclaimer
... this book ... to press. However, due to the dynamic nature of the Internet, some ... addresses ... changed, or sites may have changed or ceased to exist since publication. While the author and ... regret any ... this may cause readers, no responsibility for any such changes can be ... either the ... or the Publishers.

Contents

Words shown in the text in bold, **like this**, are explained in the Glossary.

Who was George Cadbury?

George Cadbury was one of the first people to make and sell chocolate bars. He lived 150 years ago, in **Victorian times**.

All these chocolates are made by Cadbury.

George was a very special man. He made a lot of money selling chocolate. He also did a lot to help his workers and poor people.

George built houses, schools, and hospitals for his workers.

Growing up

George was born in Birmingham on 19 September 1839. His parents were called John and Candia. George had five brothers and one sister.

This is George as a young boy (right), with two of his brothers.

George's family lived in this
house in Edgbaston, Birmingham.

George liked riding a pony and playing in
the garden. His parents were **Quakers**.
They taught George to help other people.
John ran a shop which sold tea, coffee and
chocolate for drinking.

George begins work

When George was a boy, his father opened a **factory**. He began making drinking chocolate, as well as selling it.

This is George with his father, John.

When George was 16, he went to work in the family factory. Six years later, John Cadbury **retired**. George and his brother, Richard, took over the shop and factory.

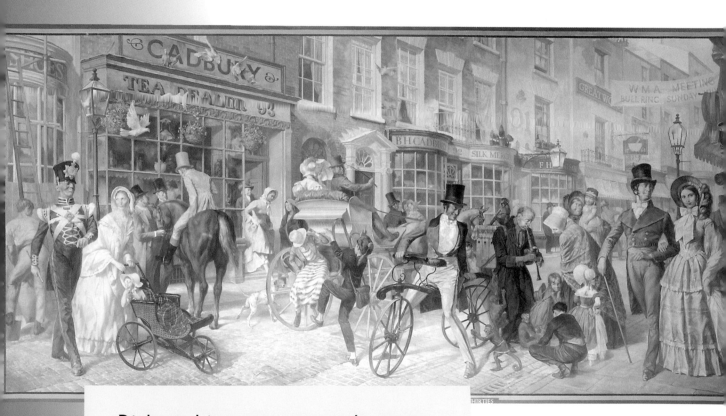

Rich and important people came to buy tea and drinking chocolate from the Cadbury shop.

The cocoa press

George began to make chocolate for eating, not just drinking. At first, it did not taste very nice. Then he bought a new machine called a **cocoa press**.

These are cocoa beans. The cocoa press squeezed the oil out of the beans and left just the **cocoa** powder.

With the cocoa press, George could make and sell '**pure**' cocoa.

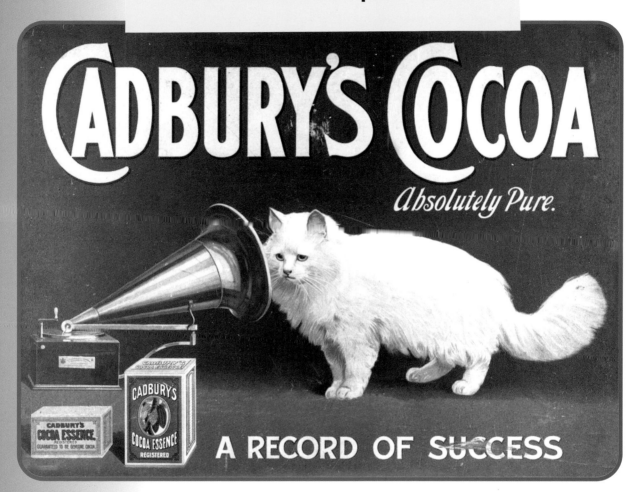

CADBURY'S COCOA

Absolutely Pure.

A RECORD OF SUCCESS

CADBURY'S COCOA ESSENCE REGISTERED GUARANTEED TO BE GENUINE COCOA

CADBURY'S COCOA ESSENCE REGISTERED

The press helped George to make better chocolate. The eating chocolate was plain and dark. It was made into bars, or used to cover fruit-flavoured centres.

Miserable lives

Most **factories** in **Victorian times** were noisy, smelly places. Men, women, and children worked for long hours every **day** in crowded rooms.

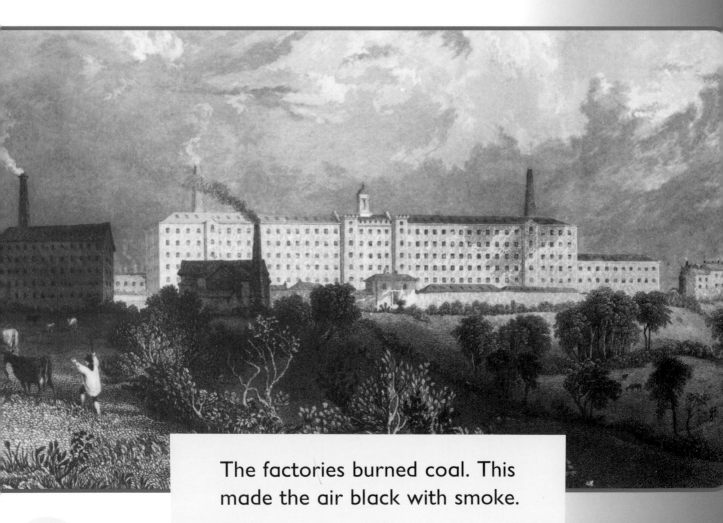

The factories burned coal. This made the air black with smoke.

The back streets of Birmingham were crowded and dirty. George saw how working people lived there. He wanted to make life better for his workers.

Big families lived in very small houses. There was nowhere for children to play.

A garden city

In 1872, George married Mary Tylor. They had five children. George wanted his workers to be as happy as he was. In 1879 he built a **factory** called Bournville near Birmingham.

George and Mary were married for 15 years. Sadly, Mary died in 1887.

In Remembrance of

MARY,

THE BELOVED WIFE OF GEORGE CADBURY, OF SELLY OAK,

WHO FELL ASLEEP IN JESUS,

AT DAWLISH, 27TH OF FOURTH MONTH, 1887,

Aged 38 Years.

The houses had front and back gardens. The workers could grow fruit and vegetables.

At the new factory, there were houses for the workers and a school for their children. There were also **washhouses** and **reading rooms**, and even a hospital.

The first boxes of chocolates

The Cadbury brothers were the first people to put chocolates into boxes – and the first to put pictures on their boxes. Each chocolate was decorated **by hand**.

Richard painted pictures of flowers, children, and country scenes for the boxes.

In the 1920s, **factory** workers still decorated the chocolates by hand.

In 1881, someone from Australia asked to buy Cadbury's chocolate. This was the first time Cadbury sold chocolate outside England.

A large family

In 1888, George married again. His second wife was called Elizabeth Mary Taylor. They had six children. Elizabeth was a good mother to all of George's eleven children.

Elizabeth did a lot to help working women and girls.

In this photo, Elizabeth and George are seated in the middle. They are surrounded by some of their children and grandchildren.

Eleven years later, in 1899, Richard died. After that, George ran the business with two of his sons and two of Richard's sons. They called it 'Cadbury Brothers Limited'.

Milk chocolate at last!

In 1897, George started making milk chocolate for eating. First he added **milk powder** to the dark chocolate, but this made it very dry. Then George tried adding fresh milk.

Adding fresh milk to dark chocolate makes it soft and creamy.

REDUCED PRICES

Half pound–2/-
Quarter pound–1/-
and 2 oz. for 6ᵈ

Cadbury's

DAIRY MILK

CHOCOLATE: 8oz

CADBURY'S MILK

FROM THE FACTORY IN A GARDEN!

This advert is from 1956. Dairy Milk adverts today still show the glasses of milk.

The fresh milk made the milk chocolate taste much better. In 1905 George made *Cadbury's Dairy Milk*. It soon became Britain's best-selling chocolate bar.

Working for others

George worked to help other people all through his life. Every Sunday morning he taught at a school for adults. **Quakers** thought everyone should be educated.

George built this school for the children of his **factory** workers.

George lived in a big house close to Birmingham. Many times a year, George invited hundreds of poor children to parties in his garden.

At George's parties, the children swam, played cricket, ran races, and had tea.

The end of a good life

As George got older, he spent more time at home with his family. He had 22 grandchildren! Many of them spent Christmas at his house every year.

This is George with one of his sons and grandsons.

George ran the Cadbury **factory** until he died in 1922. He was 83 years old. We remember him for his wonderful chocolate, and for the work he did to help other people.

The Cadbury's *Dairy Milk* wrapper used today, and the first wrapper from 1905.

Cadbury today

Cadbury still sells millions of bars of *Dairy Milk* and *Bournville* all over the world. Today, nearly 25,000 people live in the village of Bournville.

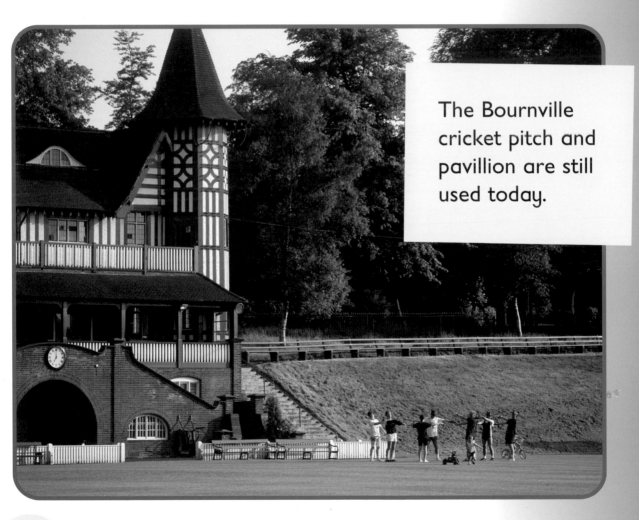

The Bournville cricket pitch and pavillion are still used today.

At Cadbury World in Birmingham, you can have fun learning about how chocolate is made. You can also find out more about George's life and work.

Cadbury World has a museum, a cinema and lots more.

Fact file

- Nearly 500 years ago, a Spanish **explorer** called Don Cortes first brought chocolate to Europe from Mexico. It was a cold, **bitter** drink so he tried putting sugar in it, and liked it.

- Some of the early Cadbury chocolate boxes were covered in velvet. Inside, there was a silk lining and a mirror.

- Cadbury was the first company to give its workers Saturday afternoon off work.

- George loved to play cricket. He sometimes played with the people who worked in the **factory**.

- The Rowntrees and the Frys were other **Quaker** families who made chocolate and sweets.

Timeline

1839	George is born in Birmingham on 19 September
1855	George leaves school and starts work
1861	George and Richard take over their father's shop and **factory**
1866	George buys a **cocoa press** from the Netherlands
1872	George marries Mary Tylor
1879	The new Bournville factory and village are built
1887	Mary Cadbury dies
1888	George marries Elizabeth Mary Taylor
1897	George starts making milk chocolate using **milk powder**
1899	George's brother, Richard, dies
1905	George **invents** *Dairy Milk* chocolate
1922	George dies on 24 October, aged 83

Glossary

advert something on TV or posters that tells people about things they can buy

bitter not sweet

by hand work that is done by a person, not a machine

cocoa powder made by crushing cocoa beans

cocoa press machine for pressing cocoa beans to take out the oil

explorer someone who travels to find new things and places

factory place where things are made by machines

invent make for the first time ever

milk powder milk that has been dried

pure not mixed with anything else

Quakers Christian group who believe they should spend their lives helping other people

reading room place where people could go to read newspapers and books

retire stop working because a person is too old

Victorian times when Queen Victoria was on the throne (1837–1901)

washhouse place where people could go to wash their clothes

Find out more

Websites

www.cadburyworld.co.uk
Cadbury World

www.cadbury.co.uk
Facts about chocolate and about Cadbury.

www.chocolateweek.co.uk
History of chocolate, plus stories and recipes.

Places to visit

Cadbury World
Linden Road
Bournville
Birmingham B30 2LD

Always remember that eating too much
chocolate is bad for your health.

Index

Titles in *The Life of* series include:

Hardback   0 431 18073 3

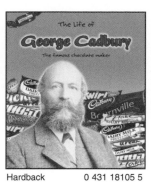

Hardback   0 431 18105 5

Hardback   0 431 18098 9

Hardback   0 431 18099 7

Hardback   0 431 18071 7

Hardback   0 431 18072 5

Hardback   0 431 18100 4

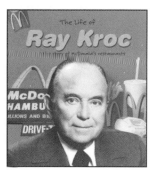

Hardback   0 431 18106 3

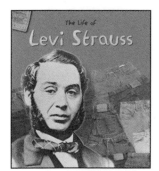

Hardback   0 431 18070 9

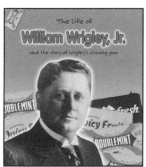

Hardback   0 431 18101 2

Find out about the other titles in the Heinemann Library on our website www.heinemann.co.uk/library